ANCHOR BOOKS

BRIDGING THE GAP

First published in Great Britain in 1994 by
ANCHOR BOOKS
1-2 Wainman Road, Woodston,
Peterborough, PE2 7BU

Foreword

Anchor Books is a small press, established in 1992, with the aim of promoting readable poetry to as wide an audience as possible.

We hope to establish an outlet for writers of poetry who may have struggled to see their work in print.

Following our request in the National Press, we were overwhelmed by the response. The poems presented here have been selected from many entries. Editing proved to be a difficult and daunting task and as the Editor, the final selection was mine.

The poems chosen represent a cross-section of styles and content. They have been sent from all over the country, written by young and old alike, united in the passion for writing poetry.

I trust this selection will delight and please the authors and all those who enjoy reading poetry.

Glenn Jones
Editor

CONTENTS

AN EXPLORATION OF SUMMER

The loony light-headed blue blinds
and sears eyes
Ecstasy rises bubbling in giddy air and trickles out
seeping through pores
Scalding skin in its haste and loss.
Each beam spears - nasty
Yet the sun's gold is craved like man's material gold.
It's all material and greed and
so crazy!
Everything is vibrant
The glossy green countryside is free
And I want it!
The paradox is freedom and captivity - life's great philosophy
And I want it!
I want cool existence. Blazing cold freedom and fluctuation
In the pulse of bloody life . . .

Rich black blood conceals its royal redness
and this doesn't bubble or escape its hot container
I want to see it stain the green -
Just a little
No pain, just gainful and free
Madness is the only true freedom - without consciousness
The chasm and void of life is found by chance
It's negative, it's death and subconscious waking
And I want it.
All of it is wrong and yet I want it all, loneliness is the
height of consciousness but extreme emotion cuts
life; lacerates its peace without mercy
I want the unattainable truth
Let it stain . . .

Nicola J Cotton

THE OLD MUSICIAN

The wind howls in the silent street
An old man walks on dragging feet
He stops at the corner and begins to play
And the tune is a melody of yesterday

His monkey prances by his side
Darting under his coat to hide
Passers by give what they can
Dropping a penny in the old tin pan

Children stop to watch the pair
The old man's face is lined with care
Remembering the time before his fall
When he played to crowds in a famous hall

That was when his Emma was near
To urge him on with a smile and a cheer
When the world applauded and called *Encore*
And he would bow and play once more

His Emma has gone and he longs for her
Sometimes the longing is hard to bear
It's time to go, so with a sigh
He turns away and whispers 'good-bye'

Through piercing wind he wanders back
To a house that's just a shack
If only his Emma was waiting there
To meet him and greet him with loving care.

E Howorth

WASH DAY BLUES

I could not get a wash today
My wife had washed the towels.
I did not get dressed today,
My wife had washed my clothes.
I had to fly around the house today,
My wife had washed the floors.
I could not have a drink today,
My wife had washed the cups.
I did not have a meal today,
My wife had washed the plates.
I had to sit on a wardrobe today,
My wife had washed the chairs.
I could not go shopping today,
My wife had washed my shoes.
I did not read a book today,
My wife had washed my glasses.
I had rubbish in my pockets today,
My wife had washed the bins.
I had to cross my legs today,
My wife had washed the toilet.
I should have stayed in bed today,
I could not,
My wife had washed the blooming bed!

D A Watson

SNAKEWOMAN

What does she have that is such a mystery
Her eyes are pale and colourless whilst
mine are brilliant blue and vibrant
Why is she so different, she has no grace
No social charms, or classic good taste

What is her power that attracts them like flies
That they hang lifeless to her every word
They see only her jiggling breasts and painted guise
If only they saw themselves - it so absurd
But he does not look at me, he lives for her

What does he see in her. I am slimmer
I do not have fat thighs, bottom or calves
I pride myself on my flat stomach - oh so trim
My exercise routine every day I never miss
Whilst she smokes, smokes and smokes

Her fag stained teeth smile from painted lips
The dyed blonde hair hangs limply down
Her mascara cakes her eyes, her powder thick and false
But he does not see me, he looks for her and smiles
I try to catch his eyes but he looks away

She wields her power like a mesmeric snake
My life she has the power to take
She asks enigmatically 'Do I want him back?'
I will not beg or plead just silently pray

But it's all in vain she spits him out
And he crawls away, pines and dies
To that she winks, slithers away and smiles.

A Nair

SEASONS

My love is the best of every season:
Mellow autumn gold; spring's majesty;
A winter rose, fair as the new May bud,
All of these, and young as summer, is she.

Oh! there never was one more lovely;
The sunlight dwells upon her face,
Resolved there to stay, held by the magic
Of her silken beauty and tender grace.

In springtime shall I romance the blossom
Of radiant love, at nature's throne,
Caressed by a rain of kisses
Far kinder than the clement sun.

I'll dread not winter the assassin
Nor summer's wistful parting sigh;
Indifference is all that I fear
In the fixed cloudlets of an eye.

Sometimes like an elusive rainbow
Is she, with fast vanishing colours,
Ever changing, and yet constant
Throughout all love's testing hours.

She is all the seasons of my heart,
The essence of light, beyond compare;
For when the crown of beauty is won,
Who would seek perfection elsewhere?

Leslie E Thomas

STARS

The gemmy suns in Orion shone
diamantine in the sky,
The boldest of all star groups bar none
now southing.

Red Betelgeuse was glowing bright
And Bellatrix nearby,
Great Rigel shining bluish-white
Saiph in attendance.

The belt of stars numbered three
the hanging sword,
Bejewelled and faint and quite misty
Great Nebula.

At Orion's heels the bright Dog Star
Faithfully following,
Shining and flashing from afar
Red, white and blue.

The evening turned to deepest night
Starry pageantry changing,
As the world revolved with all its might
New stars appeared.

Procyon, the Little Dog, came into view
And snorting Taurus,
And then there was a hint of blue
When proud Leo rose.

'Twas the dawn; the stars began to dim
Then the light, the day,
By the power of the one who's known as Him
The stars were gone.

D R Keedy

THE STRAWBERRY PICKERS

Pick Your Own the sign declares.
We go in and join the groups surveying the fields
Already dotted with stooping figures.
I choose a lane and carefully run my hands
Along the pavements of plants. Working slowly,
Picking the ones that others have left behind.
I like the smaller ones, deepest red.
To hell with tradition, eat them as they are;
Deepest red and very sweet.
We have them at home in the garden,
Not quite as big or as red,
But just as sweet.

It's a little like a treasure hunt.
Digging in the undergrowth,
Goosegrass grabbing, pulling you back,
And suddenly the sun catches one . . .
It shines like a ruby hidden in the sand.

The kids leap from row to row with cries of . . .
'Cor, look at this one. It's *GI*-normous!'
There are competitions of who has picked the most or the biggest,
When they have remembered to put them into their
Baskets and not their mouths.

I never look forward to the picking season.
It's hot and all that bending is not good for my back.
Then they charge you for bringing your own tubs!
The kids enjoy it though,
So we go every year.
I always feel I should be doing something more . . . Fruitful.

K Alexander

THE BALD TRUTH

I'm only 28, and that's not very old,
But slowly and surely I'm going slightly bald.
I look in the mirror and I stare,
At my poor old receding hair,
I look at my comb filled with dread,
It's full of hair that was once on my head!
Some people comment about the fact,
With a little smile and shortage of tact,
That my locks are going at quite a rate,
Soon I'll be left with a hairless pate,
At work I sit under a fluorescent light,
It makes my scalp shine twice as bright,
Once I would have panicked about a lack of hair,
But now I'm not so worried if it's no longer there,
Yes, it would be nice to keep it forever
But I won't wear a *rug*, no not ever!
And have it fly off on a windy day,
To be blown down the road, and swept away,
Soon I will have my own *solar panel*,
An extra bit of skin to wash with my flannel,
Is baldness really something we should fear?
Do we need to get uptight and almost shed a tear?
It's only hair, nothing more and nothing less,
And if you don't have any, it can't become a mess,
So I'll try to go bald with a little bit of grace,
And accept my new look with a smile on my face!

Stephen Norris

THE BIG DAY OUT

My daughter and I are rural types, who never see the sea,
So she suggested a train ride with her mini family.
Armed with pushchairs, nappies and milk,
Spare clothes and an extra teat,
We went to the sea with two under two's,
Believe me, no mean feat!

When we'd staked our claim for a patch by a wall,
We spread out the babies regalia.
Then we started on food and the wasps came to call,
My daughter wailed 'Oh, I'm a failure!'

Deckchairs are dangerous, so we sat on the sand,
But our charges soon became crusty,
For sand and ice-cream don't mix very well,
And the babies looked a bit rusty!

Henry's shower on the prom, along with his toys,
Was an unmitigated disaster.
He screamed with rage his 'Oh dear God' noise,
So I cleared up just a bit faster!

Then back to the station we struggled up hill
Till we found an obliging cabbie.
Henry still wet, let his drink take a spill,
Gra' explained 'he's only a babbie!'

We grimaced at fares, coped bravely with stares,
But when both babies needed a nappy,
Mum got in a stew, using the train's tiny loo,
The babies didn't sound happy!

Henry fell asleep with his head in his hands,
We relaxed with the jog of the train.
Polly stared round enjoying it all,
We'll probably do it again!

Val Bates

I AM IN LOVE

When I saw his face, I could feel the attraction, the passion
When I close my eyes, I could see his silhouette, the vision
My heart pounds every time I see him
Every moment without him has no meaning
I long for him to speak to me, touch me, kiss me
I want him to love till I can't see.

I have never felt love before,
Never felt the desire that lurks beneath.
The wave of air that brushes my face as he walks past
The feel of his presence that I hope will always last
The beautiful sensation, the intense attraction.

I cannot think of anything else except him
Just the thought of him makes my heart beam,
With delight.
His warm embrace sends tingles down my spine
Oh, when he smiles
It gives me this uncontrollable feeling,
Purely indescribable.

The eagerness, excitement of seeing him the next time
I just cannot wait to put myself in his arms again
I am without any doubt spellbound
I am highly jinxed with love

I love him and I care for him
I want this to last forever
These feelings are too precious
My darling is delicious
And so am I.

L Chevalie

DEATH

I have walked tired miles
Along hedgerows and lanes
In this home of mine
At peace with myself
Through villages of stone
Filled with concrete dwellers
I have learned to love
Rolling hills and lost meadows
In this county of the rose.

Roy Hammond

CALL FROM THE WILDERNESS

Could once again old nature grace
This mundane realm, so out of place;
Another Kipling, out there - somewhere
Who for Britain has a care.
A writer, so inspired with love of land
And children's needs, to make a stand.
A mind of substance with the human touch
To thunder words for we to clutch.
Yet, not too shy to let all know
We hold to courage, forward flow.

We sleep for want of stirring boasts
To flex the mind, shake off its ghosts;
That seem to haunt the conscience, deep
That stature bent, while round we creep.

Once, Kipling's words made men stand tall
Proud of race, attuned to call,
That soil of birth is want to make
When pride is free and steps to take.
Steps to take to right and wrongs,
The bracing march of victor's songs.
March the British way, not cowed like sheep
Afraid of all, the fear too deep.

Revigour law and just reward
Again unite - act in accord.
Shake off the cloak, assumed in shame
Resume the epic of your fame.
Let none decry your own in strife
'Tis yours to live this British life.

The book half written, many forward deeds
Still wait their turn to sew their seeds;
To sew and reap your nation due,
To truth and honour, and - to you.

Henry J Green

12

MICKEY

It stands there so sadly in the failing evening light,
Vacant eyes just staring at the very barren sight,
How could it happen that this house, once so full of joy
Could mourn so very deeply for that little white haired boy.

He happily ran around these walls always full of glee
Finding fun and excitement in all that he could see,
Little feet just racing, and eyes so very blue,
Joyfully exuberant in all that he could do.

In the front door, up the stairs, down again and out the back
Around the house, by the barn, hiding behind the haystack.
Mischievous, infectious laughter, that he couldn't hide
Always leading his sister back to his side.

Years go by and life goes on and little boys grow tall,
And everywhere he went he had a friend in all,
The magic in his fingers as he made the music play,
The joy it brought to others as they listened night and day.

Then treachery came and played a game, he couldn't understand,
In his simplicity he didn't know things so underhand,
Lies, disloyalty, betrayal and more,
Grief and pain to make his heart sore.

He tried to hide from others his sorrow and his care,
But for the ones who loved him it was very hard to bear,
For years he tried his very best though he knew he couldn't win,
How could anyone cause such anguish? What a grave and terrible
sin.

Then came a day of unbearable sorrow,
When he knew he couldn't face tomorrow,
The music stopped with a heartbreaking sigh,
The heavens cried the day he died, and so did I.

So lonely house, don't grieve now, for days that are long gone,
When all your rooms were happy with laughter music and song,
He has gone to a higher place where earth's pain has turned to joy.
But you and I will never forget that little white haired boy.

Molly Beare

THE OTHER SIDE

Why is it that the other side
always rapes, maims and kills,
Yet it's either your side or mine?
And we are friends, not enemies.
So tell me, who is the rapier,
the killer and the pilferer?
Your brother, or mine?
'It cannot be mine, he is asleep in bed!'
'It is not mine, he's eating his stew
with a chunk of bread!'
Could it be your husband, you silly fool?
Who do you call a fool?
My man's at home!
And mine won't roam.
So you see, who is the enemy you or me?
We are friends, not on opposite sides,
It must be the Blacks or the Jews,
the Irish tribe.
Haven't you seen in the news,
Blackman rapes schoolgirl.
Jews abscond with pension.
Irish kill ten with bomb.
They are somebody's
Brother, Father or Son!
I must say God, it's a strange plan.
Do you want us to murder our friends?
In your sweet fields, mountains and glens.

Jacky Monette

BLESSINGS

All the blessings I have got
Makes me feel so very humble.
To think over whilst others have not.
Who do not see but sit and grumble.

Like playing on a sandy beach
The sun is shining in the sky
My children there for me to teach
The kind of joy you cannot buy.

Peoples minds hurt and seeking,
Searching for a better way to live
Groping in the dark and reaching
Comfort healing we can give.

Those who cannot move from bed.
Their limbs imprison them so tight.
Eyes and ears heavy with lead
Long for hearing and their sight.

For brotherly love in different races.
Red and yellow, black and white
If only peace came to those places
And God's love in another light.

God is love and loves his way
Blessings shine from heaven above
So dwell in love - do what he says.
Love other people do it in love.

Margaret Davies

THE LONELY BIRD AND I

From my window I gazed at the beautiful country view,
The summer sun was shining
From a sky of crystal blue,

The trees outstretched their leafy branches of green,
Then a bird nestled on a tree,
One single bird, not another one could I see,
The bird turned its head from side to side,
but there was not another bird to perch beside,
One little bird all alone,
looking so sad all on your own,

Dear little bird I know just how you feel
I too am alone, my partner is never coming home,
dwelling beneath a summer sky,
does not bring happiness to you or I,
This earth can be a lonely place,
without the smile of a friendly face,

And so little bird if you and I
had riches untold,
A little company is worth much more,
than an empty world of glittering gold.

Patricia Campbell

PICTURES AT AN EXHIBITION

Over the mountains
Soon after tea
James drove to Lisbon
With Susanne and me.

Fed us with sweeties,
I sat in the back,
Peered through the rain
Enjoying the crack.

Parked at the gallery.
It looks very old
17th Century
Or so, I was told.

A welcoming drink
Orange or wine?
I expect you can guess
Which choice was mine.

Two huge rooms of pictures
And more on the stairs.
Susanne has sold one,
A red spot on hers.

Munching at nibbles,
I wandered around.
The one that I liked
Was £400.

Met a few friends,
Said it's time we went hame
Back over the mountains,
The way that we came.

Josephine Walker

18

BIMS WEE ACCIDENT

On these days of cold and damp
I heard you became a human ramp
I wish bim for your sake
You'd learn to pull on the tractor brake.

Now what exactly did it do?
I heard both feet were black and blue
Dad also said they were very swollen
And that Frankie stopped the tractor rolling.

Do you think these cockles are worthwhile
Driving out to sea mile after mile
Getting chilled to the bone and soaked to the skin
To earn a few pounds for a whisky or a gin.

It's Sunday today and Maxie's just gone
What he said makes me think there's nothing wrong
He said, on Saturday you had been travelling far
And had a few drinks in the Glenisle Bar.

I know you've always been a bit of a rover
And you're probably suffering from a massive hangover,
Well I suppose you've gained one thing from your treat
It'll stop you worrying about your feet.

L J McSherry

DANGER!

Harvest mouse in grass spun nest
Her thudding heart moves tiny chest,
When machine combine comes into play
It leaves her nest in disarray.

The hedgehog ambles 'cross the ground
For slugs and worms he searches round,
When dangered, rolls in spikey ball
Can he avoid the cars at all?

The strong-legged hare can he outrun
The lurcher set on him for fun?
How can they justify this *sport*?
Brave challenge them with sharp retort!

Wicked men on night-time raids
Come dig the badger out with spades,
His vocal calls, screaming and shrill
The air, his pain wracked cries do fill.

Handsome fox of fiery hue
Why do they pursue you as they do?
Fail to acknowledge vulpine grace
As dogs across the landscape chase.

Royal antlered stag of noble stance
In forest home you lord and prance,
But to sounds of hounds react with fear
Become the exhausted, cornered, hunted, deer.

Why does human contact mean such stress
They deserve our regard and nothing less,
In these creatures have some pride
Please cherish them and countryside.

Glenda Lawrence

SURROGATE PASTURES

This small borrowed lease
Of life which I claim
These few meagre moments I treasure in time
I'll travel these tradewinds and then for awhile
These surrogate pastures of earth are all mine

Each place I tread I'll borrow a dream
A renaissance with culture, a place for my soul
Each place I tread i'll leave with a tear
A pool full of memories I pinch every year

I translate the brochures
These bibles of fact
And visualise places in their glossy domain
I vanquish the winter to its contemptuous months
And welcome the ides of the summer again

I who have travelled each safari in life
Through each gothic adventure to a cultural heart
I who have sampled these national extremes
Of etiquette banquets and bedouin dreams

I've flirted with troodos
Courted life on the Rhine
And walked through the petrified streets of Pompeii
Followed the mayflower, caressed the new world
Lit dreams in the honour of each realm where I pray

I'll watch every dream from the edge of the world
And I'll barter with moments to accommodate time
I'll retreat into history and delve for awhile
These surrogate pastures of earth are all mine.

David Bridgewater

MORNING SPORT

The frosty air is crisp and keen,
The hounds impatient on the green,
The Huntsmen in their scarlet coats
Are waiting for the brassy notes
Of hunting horn, blown loud and clear,
That panics fox and hare and deer.

The chase is on, the hounds unleashed,
The horses canter o'er the heath,
A noble stag with bated breath
Takes scent of man, and dogs, and death.
Bounds from his thicket, nostrils wide,
His only thought to run, to hide.

Through field and woodland, o'er the bridge
That spans the stream at Ferny Ridge.
The stag is leading half a mile,
The hounds are gaining; at the stile
A hundred yards between them, then
The stag falls gasping in the glen.

The baying hounds of death descend,
The gentle stag meets savage end,
The hunt their mornings sport enjoyed,
The dogs and horses well deployed,
The men are pleased, their day complete.
God's creature killed - a noble feat!

R F Groves

A PLACE NAMED BASICS

Excuse me - Can you tell me the way to Basics?
They say you've all been there before.
It's an old place, just up from Bedrock,
Where they keep all their feet on the floor
It's where people call in the country,
On a day trip off *back to Basics*.
It sounds quite Anglo-Saxon -
Sussex, Basics and Essex.
Apparently, it's a haven
Where I'm supposed to run
Whenever I find I'm in trouble
And can't face up to what has to be done.

It would make a good square on a board game
- That last one before the end -
All roads lead back to Basics
So go back and start over again.

Now - about this place called Basics
That people go back to,
Has it - has it - has it got wonderful water
And - and - a completely unblemished view?
I think *Basics* the name of a holiday home
In the mind of our Prime Minister;
The message, one line on his postcard,
Says 'Oh God - I wish I was here.'

Prime Minister - The World will just not go
                backwards
- No matter how *The Old Days* look good.
And - if we could have the past, not the
                future,
I just wonder which one of us would -
I wonder which one of us would.

Arnold Owens

UNTITLED

Life is like a rose
take me let me pose
I want to fulfil your dreams
to do the things that you like most.
I may not be a model
and walk with style and grace
but it's not what's on the outside
not just a pretty face,
it's what I've got inside of me
I think that you need more
So if you'll only let me
I'll open up your door.

Helen Downes (16)

CHILDHOOD MEMORIES

Just a small cuddly puppy
Whose name tag said *Ruff*
So loved by the children
That bundle of fluff
Who would nuzzle up close
To help dry their tears
A true friend in need
To allay all their fears.

But as years have gone by
Ruff's eyes dimmed with age,
His playmates long gone
The world now their stage
Now locked in a diary
Lasting memories recall
Of a wee *pal* called *Ruff*
So faithful to all.

Sophia D Winchester

A LOVE POEM

I often glance across the room
and watch those eyes of yours.
The forest of thick, long lashes
above the dainty blue pearls.

I wonder how it would be
if you, also liked me

I then look at your face and your smile,
I know then the answer
to the question I ask.

It would be the best thing ever.
My happiness would stretch
beyond the universe and further.
Would yours?
I love you.

C Evans

TO A ROSE

Roses like velvet clean and clear
As a baby's glistening tear.
Petals smooth, with stem upright
Perfuming the cloudless night

Off the shoot a young bud peeps
Looking around while all else sleeps
Then to close its soft young eyes
Till morning gtory fills the skies

Then the sun will help it flow
Into the world a rose to grow.
Like its sisters sweet and clear,
Not a single flaw to fear.

Margaret Cullen

THE GARDEN

Lovely garden you give me pleasure
every single day
In spring you come alive in a
magical way
The daffodils, tulips, crocus and blossom
so gay
All make way for summer's most beautiful
display
Then autumn comes the leaves changing
colour, dropping on the ground to lay
Once more winter snow glistens so pretty
I must say
Oh garden so lovely may the happiness
you give me be here to stay.

F M Marriott

DREAM

Save me tomorrow for that's just a dream,
Keep all your thoughts for what might have been,
Try as you might there is nowhere to run,
Wish all you want tomorrow won't come,
Hold on to a dream that no-one can break,
No future no past nothing to take,
It's there all the time a picture so clear,
Each passing hour it's coming so near.

S Harman

STORM TEARS

Hands grasp the reins,
flowing water gains.
Glistening illuminated,
electric ice raindrops on glass.
Pitter-patter, wet shiny coated matter.
The light glows dim.
Interstellar blinking,
thinking washed away for another day.
Beacons hidden in translucent heaven,
descending from the constellation,
the starlight is real.
Window frames sealed with a vision.
Double glazed disguised in the haze.
Smiling beguiling, semi-detached,
With its gate on the latch.
A misty face conjures thoughts of theosophy.
Cracking thunder, spiting lights of fire,
leaving an empty cloud burst with feelings of hope.
A new day conceived,
the transcendental curtain unfolds,
for all this has been foretold.

Anthony Keyes

BASIC THRILLS FOR BASIC SKILLS

In our village we've had a mass meeting
To say we want high crime rate beating.
We'll put yobs in pot
Mix up ruddy lot
Then use 'em for fuel for heating.
We've all had homes burgled to core,
No pleasures of treasures no more.
Known bags snatched in shop
When will these scum stop?
Parked cars nicked, good grief, what a bore!
It's time the laws helped police get tough,
'Cos innocent folks had enough.
Let's bring back the birch
We'll not need to search,
For these yobs 'll be gone like . . . cream puffs.

Pamela Pitts

BASICALLY BACKWARDS

Back to Basics - the return.
A favourite phrase this year -
Family-ness; togetherness;
Morals of yester-year.

Bring back the old values!
True progression through the years?
Why stop at moral upbringing?
Reinvent the old ideas!

Perhaps, we should share this vision,
Just how far back should we head?
Outside, the *new* toilets wait,
Inside, lies our small brass bed (sleeps 6).

I have a dream - of flatirons;
Mangles; tin baths; gas lamps;
Electric blankets? . . . Don't be soft!
Who could mind the cold and damp?

Back to Basics - yes, of course.
Who needs their car or TV?
At home, with the wireless,
What fun . . . Don't you agree!

Donna Prime

LOST IN A DREAM

Lost in a dream
In the sky or sea
Lost in a dream.
Nothing is what it seems.
Lost in a dream
with Superman.
Lost in a dream
In no-man's land.
Lost in a dream
With no ice-cream.
Lost in a dream
With the Fairy Queen.
Lost in a dream . . .

J Jacques (13)

LOVE DENIED

I am glad I did not love you.
I am glad I did not care.
I am glad I did not need you.
For deep in my heart I know that you would not be there.

Was it true that I did not love you?
Was it true that I did not care?
Was it true that I did not need you?
Yes it was true that I knew that you
would not be there.

Pamela Venetia Orr

CONTEST

Man clashing with nature,
Coming together,
A consequence beyond comprehension occurs,
With stark brutality.

The world we live in,
The world we destroy,
Without seeming to care,
A force, nature, which does not think,
It only responds.

Its answers to correct our mistakes,
Are entirely natural,
And yet, make the situation worse,
And we realise our mistake.

The actions of a few,
Cause a chain reaction,
And many suffer,
Innocent or guilty, we all suffer,
And too few seem to care.

Seemingly helpless, we watch but do nothing,
But helpless we are not, in stopping this chain,
We choose to do nothing,
As we choose to start the chain.

The point beyond return is unknown,
We do not want to know,
And even with thought we may never know,
But there will be a point where we have gone too far,
And still too few will care.

Nature it seems, is our only hope,
And it may stop us for good,
The next generation will not know what has gone on,
They will start from nothing,
And they will not care.
Harrison Dakers

DO YOU REMEMBER

When children played happily in the park,
And elderly couples enjoyed the dark?
When folk were honest and rarely *bent*
And politicians said what they meant?

When, if you belonged to the C of E,
The local vicar popped round for tea?
When every gentleman raised his hat -
And even some doctors were slightly fat!

When days were sunny and nights were cool,
And hardly anyone owned a pool?
When, falling in love with a Cambridge *Blue*,
You had to ask *Mother* just what to do!

When, pupils for teachers had some respect,
And spelling and grammar were quite correct?
When no-one boasted, or mentioned money,
And laughed at jokes that were *really* funny?

The *good old days* when a song had tune,
And many a maiden was seen to swoon!
Perhaps you remember those far-off times -
When even *poetry* had some rhymes!

Marian Fairchild

INSOMNIA

Laying in his bed at night
He tries to fall asleep,
Longing for a woman -
Instead of counting sheep.
Sheep are rather boring
They will not jump that fence,
So he thinks about the women
With whom he wants romance.
His heart begins to quicken
As he thinks about his need,
To service all these women
By doing the *dirty deed*.
To the land of nod he drifts
Where all his dreams come true,
But waking in the morning
He finds himself black and blue.
Careless whispers whilst asleep
Doubtless caused his plight,
Trouble and strife returning
In the middle of the night.

Andy Blackwell

THE SNOWFLAKE

The journey has begun.
Towards the ground it falls.
It comes to rest,
disappearing amongst the mass,
unrecognisable as itself.

Alive only for a single moment
before it becomes lost
for eternity.
Never to return again,
in that same form.

Tracey Ross

MY VERSION OF BACK TO BASICS

We live in a different world, now 1994
Ruled by fear and violence, drugs and vice
Greed and hatred of a kind, unchecked minds cold as ice
Money and greed seem to be the theme
Profit, progress, survival, what does it all mean?
Back to basics could be good if people really understood
It does not take money to bring this about
Explanations are needed to make people understand
It is not keeping up with the Jones', new car or a house
It is real family living of caring and giving, sharing
thoughts and problems too
Being proud of each other, the old and young alike
Sharing birthdays and Xmas, holidays all in a group
Being there when you're needed , when little things go wrong
Kindness and happiness, togetherness, to belong
Knowing a love which nothing can break
Trusting each other, asking for no reward
Believing in God, thanking him in prayer
Money I know is needed to live in this world of today
Wouldn't it be a nicer world if we really tried to go back
To basics, we were born with nothing, we leave with nothing
Have a go, forget your pride.

Lena Doherty

BEING SHOT

It's unpleasant
Being a pheasant
Being shot
That's not pleasant

Being a elephant
Ivory tusks
Being shot
Bites the dust

Being a rhino
With horn
Being shot
For your horn

Being a grouse
Having no grumble
Being shot
You have no grouse

By large
Just than animal
Being shot
That's unpleasant.

E T Ward

WISHFUL THINKING

No chemical spraying on the crops.
No animal tested products in the shops.
No drugs available on the streets
No burglars performing their daily feats
All children looked after with loving care
Enough food for families everywhere
All countries living together in
Harmonious bliss
This should be everyone's fervent wish
But people greedy for power and wealth
Don't give a hoot for people's health
So Back to Basics we should go.
Will that ever happen
I really don't think so.

Jean Barr

BACK TO THE BEGINNING

Back to the beginning of the circle,
or perhaps it's the edge of a square,
it depends which way you look at it,
depends on how you stare.

It could be the start of a spiral
or the centre of a fairy ring,
to each person it's going to be different
this back to basics thing.

You may see it through rose coloured glasses
or you may not see it at all
it's according to where you're coming from
or whether you rise or you fall.

So if it's the edge of a circle
or even the centre of a square,
it's okay to go back to the beginning
as long as you know that you're there.

Paula Thomas

MADAM DORA

Madam Dora
Was a whora
Kindly reputation
Madam Dora
Kept a scora
Birds of delectation

And if you'd gorra
Hankerin' forra
Nighta fornication
Madam Dora
Had a lorra
Ways to bring elation

But to my horra
Madam Dora
Died - and consternation
How I deplora
Lossa Dora
Misery and frustration.

James L Sheehan

THE WASHING MACHINE

It stands in the kitchen, all gleaming and new,
We read the instructions to learn what to do.
The machine was created and built on the Rhine
Instructions are meant for a German fraulein!

We need a translation but the makers don't care,
So we bung in the powder and take it from there!
There are so many dials and buttons to press,
Why a red light is flashing, is anyone's guess.

We look in the window, it's all one can do,
But a wall of white soap is restricting our view
So we go off and leave it, that's the understood thing,
When the washing is finished, you hear a loud *ping*.

But something's amiss, a leak in the door?
There are waves of white foam, breaking over the floor!
We wade to the switch, and turn off the power
But the safety device makes us wait half an hour.

The clothes are dragged out, heavy, soapy and grey
And we wash them by hand, in the old-fashioned way!
The machine is still standing, its mouth open wide,
Inviting the *brave* to put more clothes inside!

Sheila McCurry

44

CANDLE-NIGHT

Late at night
I watch the candle
    Die slowly
    In the death-throes the flame
Withdrawing into
    Its body into
        Its holder into
        Nothing
Then coming again licking
The rim groping for
    Life waving around
Thrusting a moment with a spurt of strength
Like someone with cancer having a better day
    Then fainting again painfully
Just keeping alive fighting
    Impotence fighting
      Failure
Rising and
Falling hoping
Foolishly asking for more body
    From thin air with no
Response
    But a faint cheating flicker-making breath
      Dying
And trying again silently crying
    Waving and weaving
    Finally leaving
      A guttered globule
      And a spent wick.

Helen Alexander

MYSTERIES OF LIFE

In a different time, maybe in another
        place
We may have met, the path of our
        lives we trace
The start to finish, time passes
        never stops
From birth to grave, some lives touch
        but never cross

Living on emotions, make our own
        interpretations
Tears of joy, pain, searching for
        salvation
You're cast as an actor, in life's
        short play
Acts fall into places, happiness comes
        never to stay.

Scant reward from greener grass
        dreams bought and sold
Wishing on the rainbow, never to
        find that pot of gold
When cut you shall bleed, broken
        hearts always stay
Decisions that make you stronger, many
        lovers lost along the way.

You're born to die, that is the
        only answer
As the four seasons turn, your own
        grave draws ever closer
With the moon's rise and fall, fate
        declares what is to come
Passing through many changes, 'til the
        time for setting of your own sun.

Andrew Strong

46

THE GARDEN OF MY DREAM

Now one day in the garden, I was digging up a bed
When suddenly I heard voices And this is what they said:-
'I know I am a rambling rose and I am in a state.
I'd love to flower in winter alas, to June I have to wait.'
Then spoke the little snowdrop 'I'd rather stay in bed,
And show my dainty petals in the summertime instead.'
The daffodils and tulips thought they'd like a change from Spring.
The wallflowers and the forget-me-nots thought summer was
the thing.
I know if I'm not dreaming, what a state we'll all be in.
For looking in the garden we won't know what month we're in.
I'd love to know what happens beneath the warm brown soil.
How do the plants know when it's time for them to start and toil.
It is a mystery to me, how nature knows just when
To tell the plants, get on your skates, it's flowering time again.
I think it must have been a dream I could have gone to sleep.
I'm very glad to know that now the seasons are complete.

Joan McQuoid

CLIPPIN'

They clippit the sheep oan oor ferm the day
Noo that we've seen the last o' May.
There wis Bob and Eck and Jock and Jim,
And puir wee Bess wis kept oan the rin.

The power wis switched oan, the shears started tae go,
And within twa meenits, wee Bess had tae go,
Wi' fingers and thumbs all o' a flutter,
I wis shair I could hear her gie a loud mutter.

Wi' twa oan the clippin' their backs gettin' ratchet,
It ta'en pair auld Bob, the ewes tae get catchet.
'Oh, widn't it be braw' he wis sayin' tae his sel',
'If they auld ewes wid lie doon by theirsel.'

There wis nithin' but wool fleein' through the air,
Bein' thrown oan the groon frae they clippin' pair.
Fa'in doon, oan the wrang side instead o' the richt,
Ye've niver seen sic a sicht.

Noo ye've tae stairt frae the end and work yersel' up,
Throwin' in frae each side and hopin' fer luck.
When it's a' rowed up and intae a baw'
That there's enough at the neck end tae keep it anaw.

Aboot a hunder and ten sheep later,
Ye get tae a stage whaur it disnae mater.
If it wis tae rain, wee Bess widna' greet,
'Cause she's been fair rin aff her feet.

But ye ken, I can mind in days gone by
When I wis only aboot knee high.
Ma faither did it a' by hand oan his ane,
And I rowed the fleeces if I wis at hame.

J Melville

48

FREEZE-UP

Outside my kitchen window, in the fog and frost and snow,
　There's a raucous war a-waging for the food I've thrown below.

The Rooks and Gulls are fighting; They interrupt my writing.
　There's a Blackbird and a Pigeon shadowboxing by the wall.

While underneath their noses, with scorn for warlike poses,
　A pair of Robins make a tasty meal and a Sparrow hops in and out
　　　　　　　　　　　　　　　　　　　　　　　　　to steal.

There's a Wagtail to and fro-ing, a Finch with breast a-glowing,
　A flock of Starlings swooping down to call.

The Orange Cat wakes and stretches; seems to say - 'Such noisy wretches!'
　Goes out to test the snow with cautious paw.

And so - he ends my party! The birds rise up and go.
　To them he personifies - The Foe.

So - I'm left, with leg in plaster - horrible disaster!
　To wait for freedom - and the thaw.

Mary Agnes Elliott

EGGER AND THE BEGGAR

The West wind doth blow
In May we'll have snow
And what will poor Hexham do then, do then?
For the snow will be blue
And clogged up with glue
Which poisons both beasties and men, Ye ken.

When Jenny was wed
Everyone said
How fair was the prospect in view, in view
Till with wild surmise
This smoke met their eyes
They realised the warnings were true, they knew.

So now when you look
Take bell, candle and book
And promise to fight to the end, the end
So that menacing Egger,
Like John Major's beggar,
The eyes of good men shan't offend, offend.

Lavinia Orde

THE SHOPPIE DYKE

Oh! What a lovely sunny day
Time for us to go out to play
Past the Strombinda and Groat's old yacht
Wondering how many crabs we had caught
A look in their purses not much fun
The sky is so blue and what a warm sun
Our feet are bare and a mop of red hair
Wondering what more we can find to share
We lived and we played down on the shore
Never thinking there was anything more
Over we went to The Shoppie Dyke
Empty tins we gathered with all our might
Now we had a counter and a chip shop
Loads of things found on the beach that was our stock
The sea was the vinegar the sand was the salt
From the shingle what a chips we all got
The counter was called The Shoppie Dyke
To us I can tell you it was a wonderful sight.

Marie Foulis Kennedy

51

IT'S FREE!

When the holidays are over, the sales will soon be on,
Some just go window shopping, 'cause the money's nearly gone,
They're hunting for a bargain, as they go rushing into town,
And they're eyeing up the merchandise, as they go browsing round.

A video recorder, or maybe a CD.
Some think things make them happy, but how foolish they can be
I've found the greatest bargain, that man has ever found,
No need to book provisionally, there's enough to go around.

It doesn't run on batteries, or *Electricity*,
It even comes direct to you, with a lifelong guarantee,
What is this thing? I hear you say, I'd like to have it too,
But when I tell you what it is, I wonder, what you'll do.

It's a thing that's called Salvation, and it's absolutely *Free*!!
Christ paid the price on Calvary, when he died for you and me
So get down on your knees today, and before your Maker call,
Just ask him to forgive you, for sins both great and small.

He'll give you joy in heart and soul, he'll give you peace of mind
But happiness within this world, my friend, you'll never find.
We all need this Salvation, just try it and you'll see,
You'll have such happiness within for all *Eternity*.

Shirley Snowden

SHINGLE AND SHORE

Oh come with me to the sunlit sea
To the rock strewn sandy shore.
We will chase the waves and explore the caves
With sea-green, shell strewn floor.

In his rocky pool
The crab sits still
Awaiting the incoming tide.
And anemones too, of brilliant hue,
Cling to the grey rock side.

Where the seaweed green and the brown sea wrack
By the waves are playfully flung.
Where the seagulls screech and the wind blows fresh
Come now, say you'll come.

Sybella Connell

AUTUMN LEAVES

Autumn leaves are falling; falling fastly falling,
Autumn leaves are scattered, as winter is calling,
Autumn leaves are stiffening, stiffening with the frost and rain;
Autumn leaves are dying, as winter comes again

Autumn leaves in forests and in streets, here and there,
Shall soon be swept by autumns breezes and scattered everywhere
Autumn leaves bring sadness as trees are torn bare,
Leaving ghostly stiffened figures in the frost bitten air.

Leaves of golden brown, orange, yellow and red,
Closely packed together, rotting in a frosty bed,
Leaves all shapes and sizes lie still in the chilly night,
Alone with the stars in heaven and their bright twinkling light.

Kieran Doyle

LOVE IS ALL AROUND

We met with our eyes and we reached for the skies
and without a doubt it was with no surprise.
So we phoned with a tone in the wee little hours
and soon we were to meet but it was with a cheat.
As the weeks go by you are always on my mind
but I can't help thinking that *Love is All Around.*

Dipping and driving to be with you
gives it so much pleasure when I do see you.
Soon we were to meet by the hot glowing fire
with caressing and touching until our hearts desire.
Soft breathing, parting talking was enough to mute the silence.
So whenever the small hours come, we found it hard to unchain
but I can't help thinking that *Love is All Around.*

Love is All Around as the torch is always lit
but time will tell if the ring will fit.
So we stand side by side,
With decisions awaiting on our new beginning
unhappiness and sadness were soon to set in
but not without a tear and not a grin
Finally we let go and soon guilt and morning were staring
but I can't help thinking that *Love is All Around.*

P McAlister

ROMANY WAYS

Along a dark and dusty road,
A group of people with no fixed abode
Search for a place to stay the night
With nothing to guide them but the moonlight.

Horses are tethered, a campfire is lit,
They've found a place they can stay for a bit
For some of the night they dance and they sing,
With not a care in the world of what tomorrow may bring.

Night soon turns to morning, and daybreak has begun,
All the gypsy children awake with the morning sun,
They dance, and they play in the open air
They live for today, for tomorrow they don't have a care.

The next day they move on not knowing where they will stay for the
night
A trail left by the colourful wagons is all that remains in sight,
People and places may change and be gone,
But Romany Ways will live on and on . . .

Mary Stewart

A ROSE AND A TEAR

A tear fell from my eyes
And my heart cries
A rose and a tear
That comes once every year

In a garden grows a rose
It was the fairest in the land
I tended it morn til night
But soon it passed away from sight

Now there falls a tear
On your grave that's so bare
No-one comes to see you
And you're lonely and blue

Now there is a tear
Where the rose lies
More beautiful in death
Than you were in life

If I could return yesterday
I'd pray for you and that sad day
But we can't live two days in a row
And my heart cries with sorrow.

A Mackintosh

THE LEAVING

The time had come for you to leave
And you did leave but took no leave

When you left and thus did leave
There was nothing left but me to leave

When you left and thus were gone
There was nothing left to be among

Nothing left not e'en a hair
No perfume left that clung to air

Nothing left I do declare
How do I know you had been there

You did leave of that I'm sure
Memories fade though still endure

The time had come for you to leave
Yet when you left you took no leave

It was as if you might come back
Although you had no thought of that

The time had come for you to leave
And you did leave but took no leave.

Dawn Souter

STORM BREWING

Storm brewing
Upon the horizon
Ships sailing,
Shift and sway,
Oh, how I wish
The wild wind blowing
Would blow all our troubles away.
Waves crashing
Upon the rock face.
Up leaps the white foaming sea.
Women weeping,
Hearts turn with sorrow,
Wondering why their loved one should die.
Children sleeping,
Tomorrow's people.
Are they destined for more?
Storm brewing -
Troubled waters
Converge on a troubled shore.

Clive Jackson

ALL OUR YESTERDAYS

You may be gone but you haven't left
Your gentle kindness I can't forget
For like summer's sun you warmed my heart
Your smile kept sadness far apart
Your silent voice will never stray
I know I'll hear it every day
The birds for you will sing a lullaby
I'll bow my head and gladly cry
When morning breaks and the night is gone
They'll sing again their loving song
With angels wings I shall watch you fly
Through sunbeams dancing round the sky
You have passed and left us all
For you had to follow heaven's call
Meadows green and rivers deep
On clouds of silk I know you sleep
Yet in my heart I pray you might
Fill my darkness with your light
New born baby's cries shall be
You crying out to me
For when in death life shall seed
Past is future the path you lead
You have left me all alone
Within the four walls of your home
No more to hear your wise old ways
Memories lost of yesterday.

James Kershaw

CREATIONS OF GOD

Thank you God for making trees
For creating flies and honey bees
Thank you God for making plants
For creating moths and big black ants
Thank you God for making flowers
For making the minutes and all the hours
Thank you God for creating friends
For creating things, the list never ends
But thank you God for making something to be
God I thank you for making me.

Eileen Dorgan

THE WITCH

As the mist swirled round in the gleam of the moon
A witch rode by on a long handled broom
She cackled and crowed through the night as she rode
And clinging behind her a saucer-eyed toad.

At break of day I espy
Her ghostly silhouette etch the sky
Swooping and spinning thru' shrouded space
Riding the West Wind she travels apace.

On the leeward side of the barren hill
In the depths of the forest silent and still
There looms a sombre Gothic Hall,
And there she lurks till twilight fall.

Nora McCarthy

WEATHER OF THE MIND

As the sun eclipsed the moon,
Long shadows fell over the room,
Stillness has overcome this moment in time,
The dust gathers on the picture frame,
Outside a bird sits on the window pane,
It's singing, chirping as it feels no worry,
Only the breeze on its delicate wing.

Looking out the misty window,
Observes the gathering of clouds above,
Rain falls from the sky,
As does teardrops from my eye.
I tried to turn my back on this,
Yet I stop and hesitate.
For I notice a reflection on the glass,
Of a face from my past.

I turned around to provide a kiss,
Yet you were not by my side.
A mere figment of my imagination.
I clung to the pillow,
And then began to cry.
As the clouds of thought gathered in my mind,
I tried to escape this hidden pain.

But it seemed all was in vain,
For there is no escaping memories,
There is no shelter from the rain.

D Gray

ME THE OLD PERSON

Me the old person watching
My years go by,
Thinking of my childhood
and how I'm going to die.
As I look out my window
and see the children play,
I am very thankful for
yet another day.
I wonder if they'll tend
me, in my days ahead,
And come when I am
sick lying in my bed.
And when the day has
come for me to go away,
I'll think of the children
I thank you is what
I'll say.

Siobhan Rice

COMPLAINING

Will I always be alone?
Will I always be afraid?
Will I always be cold on a hot
                    summer's night?

Through tearstained eyes
            I see happiness
Through clenched fists
            I embrace their love
Through a painted face -
    Do they see my fake smile?

Will anyone ever love me?
Will anyone ever hold me?
Will anyone ever touch me?
Or am I destined for a world
                    of loneliness.

Deborah Matchett

AGAINST THE ODDS

I am sick of jokes and twee replies about
missing socks.
Fact is, I have eleven odd ones.
It's not funny, amusing, diverting,
Guardian letters-page, Radio 4 humorous.
It's deeply bloody annoying.
I am angry about socks.
When it comes to the dying of the light I shall rage
against the losing of my socks.

They are not a metaphor for anything.
They don't make a statement about anybody's life.
They are literal, serious lost items.
Like breaking your arm in the toilet,
dropping, and smashing, a bottle of wine,
shitting in a bidet by mistake,
are not fucking funny.
Anyone who thinks they are is asking
to be choked
with eleven odd socks.

Brian Mawhinney

PRIMROSES

Yellow petals,
Leaves of green,
Grows under bushes
Hardly seen.
Delicate perfume,
Feels like velvet,
The last of Winter's frosts
Don't harm it
Scattered over
Woodland bare,
Heralds spring
Every year.
Gathered by children
For their posies,
Small and fragile
Sweet primroses.

Joan Jemson

WHAT IS A HOME?

A home is a place filled with love every day,
Where people are happy to sit, talk or play.
It's a place for relaxing, for being at ease,
For putting your feet up, doing just what you please.
It's a place made for laughter, for giving and sharing,
And what's more important, for loving and caring.
Once I had a home, it was cosy and fine,
But now things have changed and it's no longer mine.
Now I don't belong there, I find that hard to forgive,
I don't have a home, just a place where I live.

June Stokes

WHAT DOES IT MEAN?

Endless lines of nothing,
Thoughts that wander by,
For a moment they're important,
But I don't realise why.

Dreams and visions changing,
With every second past,
Scattered thoughts recalled,
That differ from the last.

Why do women have the babies?
Why do peer groups influence?
What makes a person lonely?
Teaching spells experience.

Life's too short to argue,
Why must we all compete?
Does love ever prosper?
Why do we have two feet?

If Jesus was our saviour,
Why the heartache and the pain?
Society expects the norm,
And don't hesitate to complain.

How can a world of harshness,
Say selfishly 'Oh well,'
If there really is a heaven,
Then down here must be hell.

Sarah Maycock

LINDA'S SONG

The headstrong man did fail to listen
carelessly determined in what he should rightly deserve
A sudden crushing realisation and what now is missing
to recall those softly spoken heartfelt words.

Music and memories fail to heal such particular pain
the inner most feeling contained within the darkest of letters
A struggle for composure and lengthy walks in sunshine and rain
without warning it steals upon you how can I forget her.

Even good old time failed to discover the true meaning
when those eyes betrayed bitter disappointment and surprise
The conclusion being that he was not what he seemed
it had to be perfect beneath such is the act of disguise.

David Cooper

MOUNTAINS TO CLIMB

I love you, yet I am afraid of you,
I know not when the sun will smile across
                              your brow
Or dark clouds will break over your
                              craggy face.

I am hypnotised by your awesomeness,
Yet aware of your unpredictfulness,
When I am with you, there is anticipation,
Of your countenance changing to storm,
When I am away from you I long for the
                    comfort you bring,
You are my drug; once consumed you are
                    there in my body
Intoxicating me to a fever with admiration,
For the feeling it brings I do not want to
                    withdraw from,
You are the balm onto my troubled soul.
I will always hurry back to you,
For to wander no further
To seek no more for better,
As where could I find such sweet contentment
As wrapped here, in your beloved folds.

Rotha Mulvihill

PASSING ON

The night
had almost come
and
the rain had not ceased
among the hills
of an unknown *land*.

Behind
twelve miles away
of
desolate sky peace
a village deep
of a landlord's *hand*.

Before
were three houses
on
a mile of deep lanes
an inn, a church
and a parson *grand*.

I chose
the inn's solace
of
a room with good beer
and a great fire
with a hostess *round*.

Next day
after praying
I
walked twenty miles long
on roads gleaming
and grey moss and *mound*,
dreaming . . .

Ray Nurse

NURSERY RHYMES FOR THE 1990'S

Little Miss Muffet
made a big profit
from selling her curds and whey
a spider came prying
she said, 'Are you buying . . .?
it's on special offer today!'

Little Jack Horner
sat in the corner
playing with his Nintendo
his sister was sighing
his brother was crying
'cos they wanted to have a go

Mary had a little lamb
she kept it in her flat
she stuck some paper whickers on
and pretended it was a cat

Her landlord was not easily fooled
and said it had to go
he said that cats do not possess
a fleece that's white as snow

So Mary had no home again
and was feeling rather low
for everywhere that Mary lived
the lamb just had to go!

Loraine Jane Banner

NO FLIES ON LLOYD GEORGE

Radicals with balls of fire
Stick in the mire,
Resigned to be
The runners-up, the shadow men,
The deputies.

Those today who would aspire
To higher office,
Must be filed:-
As smooth as Smith, as bland as Blair,
As Major mild.

Do they have to be so *Nice*,
So free of vice,
So goody-goody?
I would prefer prime-ministers
With redder blood.

Where are the leaders with charisma
Like Lloyd George
With lots of spunk?
But wait a minute whilst I ponder -
Didn't Paddy dunk?

Norman Bennett

SCHOOL DAYS

Blue school knickers, Fair isle tops,
Shoes that don't fit, and handknitted socks,
The smell of school dinners, the stomach would heave,
Some we would eat, and some we would leave.

Discipline was strict, the school we did fear,
Come Monday morning, produced many a tear,
Name riddled desks, and inkwells to fill,
The choosing of prefects, befitting the bill.

Hard sticks of Liquorice, Cinnamon sticks,
Sharing your lollies, each taking licks,
Sharing your chewing gum, also your comics,
We shared almost everything, even bad stomachs.

To see old Mother Riley, on the pictures we'd go,
With anticipation to see all the show,
We'd boo, and we'd yell, and we'd stamp our feet,
If the picture broke down and spoiled our treat.

Threepence on front row, a penny at back,
So many kids you couldn't keep track
Roy Rogers for lads, Walt Disney for lassies,
The girls eyeing the lads, and them making passes.

Free school milk, Brown woolly tights,
We must have looked some horrible sights,
Aye, we liked it best when school was through,
Then nobody told us what to do.

Jean Little

CAVE IN

In the dark on my own
got to keep awake
with the tears and the sweat
making pools on the floor
I can think
Time passes here I sit
hoping someone will come
trying to hold back choking screams
in the silence of the tomb
How long since the roof caved in
Too dark to see my hand
Can't move my legs but feel the pain
an ever tightening band
Mustn't sleep, to sleep's to die
need listen for some sound
something to tell me help is coming
not forgotten underground
but nothing stirs just far away
across the tunnel floor
water dripping lands beside
the drip that dropped before.

J W Wallace

THE MARKET TRADER

I stand in the Market place
Selling my wares.
Custom is bad
Nobody cares
How us humble folk
Make a living
They stand and watch
To see if I'm giving
My special once a week offer.
I soon draw a crowd
When there's something to give
How is a poor bloke supposed to live?
When nothing goes into the *Coffer.*
Stay for a while,
Have a good look
By Something! If it's only a book.
'Come on Lady, what do you need?'
I've plenty of bargains
If you care to heed
All the things I have to say.
'Come on Lady.' It's bargain day.'

Evelyn A Evans

VICTIMS

The cornflower and poppy growing side by side,
Fed richly by the blood of the many men that died,
They died in their thousands, killed by shot and by shell,
Each one living through his own private hell,
They cowered in their trenches away from bullet and blast,
Each one knowing that this breath could be his last,
They marched off to battle to a glorious tune,
To a landscape, that was cratered like the dark side of the moon,
They advanced bravely with no thought to retire,
And died hanging like specimens on the bloody barbs of wire,
They died in their thousands before each setting of the sun,
Without hope or dignity in their fight against the gun,
They marched forward bravely to a future uncertain and unknown,
And died without even their name upon a stone,
They are remembered only by family and friends,
Each a victim of man's stupidity which never ends,
This conflict was called by many the war to end all wars,
But many more are in the world like running, open sores.

Christopher Newmarch

AUTUMN

Without autumn there would be
no spring or summer,
a disaster for every country lover,
hedgerows with their rich mantle
of scarlet hips and haws,
providing food or a remedy for sores,
the bramble is in full blossom
a feast for squirrels and birds,
plums full of drowsy wasps
sleeping unperturbed,
grapes are ripe and ready for gathering,
birds migrate to distant shores,
ash keys await a spring scattering,
another of mother nature's chores.

B J Harrison

FLORAL TRIBUTES

That single rose given from his heart,
a dozen, when we had to momentarily part.
A bouquet to welcome our treasured new daughter,
a bunch, for saying things he ought not to!
Long stemmed roses complete with champagne,
to hide his guilt, causing me such pain.
That bunch of violets from a Paris street seller,
the affair over, but he couldn't tell her.
A mixed bouquet without a card,
leaving us, for her, I know it was hard.
Another single rose, delivered to my door,
he loved us, always had, my heart felt sore,
then a dozen, tied with red ribbon,
to celebrate his return, all is forgiven,
life turns full circle, to forgive is divine?
From that day twenty years ago with that gift of a rose,
then he was mine, as now, like his floral tributes,
his love grows and endures what about me? My thoughts? I'm mute,
negative thoughts I push to the back of my brain,
I pray he'll never send me long stemmed roses, ever again!

Joyce Hefti-Whitney

WILD AND RUGGED

A wilderness in the heart of Devon
Our national park, a piece of heaven
Rolling hills and granite Tors
Full of legends, that's our moors.

A rugged beauty, sometimes bleak
Intriguing tales for us to seek
Nature trails, a water fall
Ancient woodlands, trees so tall.

Ponies born free, windswept, wild
Sheep and cattle, roam meek and mild
A clapperbridge, white gurgling water
Spectacular areas to picnic or saunter.

Archaeological interest, still to explore
Bronze artefacts, traced for sure
Evidence too of primitive hut circles
Relic remains of tin mines, and ghostly echoes.

Shirley Sperry

ALLOWING TO DREAM

I'm allowed to think
I'm allowed to dream
I'm allowed to wander
What might have been?

I could have said yes
Yet I said no
A fool who pushed away love
I'm the fool who let you go.

I think of you
I dream thoughts through the day
If I saw you now
I wonder what I'd say.

Around the world
Over the moon we'd dance
If my love could find you again
If I was allowed a second chance.

I can sit and think
And be allowed to dream
Of a beautiful love
That could have been.

C Clynch

LOST GENERATION

A boy lays in the gutter
A needle by his side
A life so short a last resort
He even lost his pride.

He lived without a future
Then he died without a life
He will never know the happiness
Of children and a wife.

They say it will not harm you
They say you will feel no pain
For they know once you try it
That you will be back again.

For a pusher makes a million
He will make it out of sorrow
Another trip, another hit
Another death tomorrow.

John F Connor

OH WHAT A BORE!

There she goes again
Off to the village store
Through sun, wind or rain
This is her daily chore.

'Hello I'm off to buy a packet of tea,
Don't like this weather, do you?
It'll be straight home again for me.'

Sitting,
Sipping her tea, she looks around,
Wondering what next to do.
I know she thinks, I'll go to the store,
I could do with a biscuit or two.

Fussing, grumbling, all day long,
Back and forth she goes,
This sad and lonely old lady,
All the village knows.

That's her way of life,
Trudging from home to store,
There and back again,
Once more.
Day in, day out, always the same,
Oh what a terrible bore!

Marina Hargreaves

DISTANCE

The miles between us is so far
Even though we use a car
Feelings stay as you leave
Wishing you were here.

Tears flow because we're sad
Thinking of the friends we had -
In a precious mam and dad
Wishing you were here.

Only if the time would pass
Quicker than an hour glass
We would smile, because we knew
That we'd once again see you.

Memories linger, fond and true
Of the things we did for you
But even better are the thoughts
Of the things you do for us.

Thank you both you're very kind
Thinking of us all the time
And we think the world of you
Doing things you shouldn't do.

Sad you've gone, and we're parted
All of us are broken hearted
Till we meet again once more
We'll *keep a welcome* at our door.

D Roderick

A TEENAGERS ADVICE TO PARENTS

Teenage years are painful
Needing lots of care
So here's some helpful hints
For all mums and dads to share.

Now that I'm growing up mum,
Try your best to see
Cuddles just aren't macho
They don't suit the teenage me.

Good parents always humour
Little teenage quirks
Choose designer labels
And not Marks and Spencer shirts!

I'd like to raise the question,
Hope you won't be sore,
Would you mind just leaving
Shirts and trousers on the floor?

Perhaps you'd speak to dad,
Get him to agree
If friends come to visit
It means breakfast, lunch and tea.

When teenage blues engulf me
Causing endless grief.
Patience failed? Tempers frayed?
You'll find a tenner brings relief.

Lorraine Wyie

RWANDA

I would like to help your refugees
As many are plagued with disease
Thousands die everyday
Many leave us the same way.

War and disease pollute their land
Friends and foes give a helping hand
Terrorists and crooks stand together
To make the people have fearful hearts forever.

They inflict pain on their fellowman
And suppress the government if they can
United Nations come to their aid
But all hopes are starting to fade.

Many families have lost loved ones
Mothers, daughters, fathers even sons
Like leading young lamb to the slaughter
The rebels kill a family with a mortar.

The refugees flee the country to Zaire
To the haven in Goma which is near
Can you help these people in despair
If you do we know you care.

Paul Simms

DON'T WASTE MONEY ON A HORROR MOVIE

Take a second to think deeply, to look close, imagine far.
Know that your life is *here* - wherever you are -
And it isn't too often you force open your mind
To other places and lives of a frightening kind.
You see it in the papers and hear it on the news
But flicking your hand enables you to remove
The images of death, destruction, despair,
Pain of everyday scenes to thousands over *there*.
The world is one planet, many people, but a whole;
Yet we stay *here* disgusted to know *there's* also home.

Catherine Roberts

ABORTION

White sheets, white walls, white ceiling
White pillows to cradle my spinning head
So tired, so weary, so sick, so ashamed
Eternal tears and wishing I was dead.
Maybe in time, senses will return
In time the mind and body will forget
The white purity of this room
The void in my soul, black as jet.
I'm alone again now - just me.
Nothing inside me, fighting for life
Gone, discarded, pulled from me
Torn and disposed of by a sanitised knife.
Will I love again, feel anything again
Will tears and anger ever disappear
Will I trust again and will I walk again
Into any man's arms without fear.

Gill Oliver

SALT WATER

The sea is so blue it looks red
as it licks guest houses from the
shore like ice-creams,
snatching them off the counter with
foaming tongues and dragging them
down a mute gullet,
where the mullet fly in the cupboards
and up the stairs and into rooms that
glow in young memory.

The attack is over,
the attic is their oyster as they flutter
among its sprawling litter and muffled
pieces of old parlour conversation that
loom and blend with iron-grey sky overhead,
and how many dreams were incubated?
Caught by the tender sleep of those just wed,
whose post-consummated fray is over now the
wet patch is a mile deep.

Lee Chapman

TEMPTATION

Dare I touch it, turn and see,
is there anyone watching me?
All excitement, all aglow,
stretch my fingers, here I go.
Touch it, feel it, oh what fun,
my adventure's just begun.
If I stretch a little more,
I know I'll get it to the floor.
Oh, but who is that I hear,
could that be mummy standing near.
'Not to touch it,' did she say,
please, please mummy go away.
Can't you see I'm having fun,
today you know that I've reached one.
I can stand now, can't you see,
this is waiting just for me.
Please, please mummy go away,
let me get on with my play.
Turn once more, I can see,
she's no longer watching me.
Stretch my fingers just once more,
there, I knew, I'd get it to the floor.
Now I've got it, oh what glee, but,
is it really meant for me.
Now I have it, I'm not sure,
that I want it anymore.

C Davis

EGO

Ego's come in all shapes
Lifting ideals that hardly work
Musicians casualties of their own plight
Weekender's drink, some fight.

Monday arrives, politicians take their seats,
Out of control ego's argue five days a week
Products of TV fame believe viewers are in for a treat
Criticism is more at its peak.

Money plays its part, cars millions must have, some talk.
Advertisement points hurry and buy who wants to walk
Following these illusions so many will fall
Humble a few stand tall.

Alan Jones

CRUEL DISEASE

Cruel disease.
Cruel disease.
Which is worse, aches, pains or broken knees?
To see suffering abound
Wherever it is found,
Can be o so chiiling
Totally unfulfilling.
Sympathy never felt or heard
Compassion ever lost in word.
Condoling responsiveness hidden
Heart-heartedness is the beast that's ridden.
Sorrowful dejection experienced in suffering
Lamentable grief is the constant buffering.
Who is the loser in this ongoing war?
Woeful one who will easily deplore?
The heart of a beast, the heart of a god,
The one whose back is broken by strapping rod.
Cruelty begets cruelty and kills us all
Who knows when the next in-valid will fall.
Worthless cruel disease,
Brings us all to broken hearts, broken knees.

Denise Shaw

THE ROSE

The rose the queen stands all supreme,
in her garden realm near lawns of green.
From her stems of sharpened thorns,
little buds in spring are born.
Each one grows with grace and shape,
the petals neatly in their place,
Perfumed and soft as a maiden's face.

The sadness then we see as on its way to rest,
Petals lay upon the ground in memory of its dress.
Its petals fall like teardrops,
from a bride who never wed.
The silken rose of loveliness
like confetti now is spread.
But in its hour of sadness
spring will bring warm rain,
The rose and all its beauty
will bloom in gardens once again.

V N King

THE WAITING YEARS

Someone to hug, or someone to hold
Someone to warm me when I am cold,
A kindly glance, a deepening wish
For the smallest, briefest, friendly kiss.
A hand to hold, an arm to grasp
Safely enfolded within firm clasp,
A smile so warm and arms so strong,
To soothe and comfort when things go wrong.
The years we had, were made of gold
Until you went, then I knew the cold
On loneliness, sorrow, night after night,
I've tried, how I've tried, with all of my might
To shake off the dread, to go out and live
But, how, where, now I've nothing to give?
My heart was with you, for so many long years,
Now, I've nothing at all left, nothing but tears.
I've passed every day since that day that you died
Alone in the cold, I've wept and I've cried.
I'll wait, then I'll go, when the call comes for me
Willingly, then forever, together we'll be.

Margaret Laws

BEDROCK

I'll tell you the truth, and it's all about bed,
Because, on this subject there's lots to be said
Small, inexpensive, or dear and extensive,
All of our lives are wrapped up in our bed.
The first great occasion is our natal day
Nurse or the midwife will bear you away
Happy relations and grins from the quack
Later in life we all try to get back.
It's there for hangovers and lovers and *flu,*
Its four legs are there for the use of our two,
Laugh there and cry there, lucky ones die there,
No sleeping bag can compare with that bed.

Angie Von Tobel

KARLA, MY GORGEOUS WIFE

When I hold you, close to me,
It's like a warm wind, over the sea,
When I kiss you, I close my eyes,
It's like floating up in the skies.
When I touch you, so tenderly,
You fill my heart, with sincerity,
When I hold, your little hand,
It's like touching sun warmed sand,
When I see your pretty face,
It's like a flower, and pretty lace,
You have a warmth, that glows with light,
It touches my soul, day and night
I love you so much
That words cannot say
I could not live without you
For even a day.

My heart is yours forever.

John May

THE SONG OF CARIDWEN

I am the seed that you sow.
I am the bird on the wing.
I am the hen in the meadow.
I am the divine song that you sing.

I am the goddess of light and of dark.
I am the goddess whose bird is the black crow.
It was I who put the song, in Taliesin's heart.
I am the goddess of the white sow.

I am the guardian of the cauldron.
I am the crone, I am the mother.
I am the guardian of great wisdom.
I am the earth, I am the ruler.
I am the *goddess*, I am Caridwen.

Daniel Bran Griffith

RELIGION

Each day our faith leads us forward,
To try and reach our goals,
Knowing you are with us on this hard road,
Give us courage and faith as we go.

Knowing your God, understands us
Helps us grow, from within,,
Having that love, helps you with everything you do,
He gives you strength and courage,
To face our trails ahead
Never being alone or afraid, for he is with us.

No matter what religion we are,
We all strife to reach our God,
Try and do what our faith asks of us,
We all want to believe in the good, in mankind,
Our faith, protects us from evil all around us.

For we are all God's children,
He excepts us for who we are,
He forgives us our failings, and weaknesses,
We do not have to prove ourselves to him.

He is the father of all fathers,
He loves us all,
No limits are set by him,
He gives us unquestionable love,
What more could one ask for,
From ones religion and faith.

D Blowers

A WELSH PICTURE

St David's Day
Daffodils, leeks,
Children eagerly singing Welsh songs,
In costume,
Tall black hats, edged with lace,
Red flannel petticoats
Aprons and shawls.
Smiling faces, women,
Cockles in wooden tubs,
And a song to the morn.
Choirs, organs and a gentle harp,
The ebb and flow of rich, deep voices
In the halls of music.
The beauty of nature,
Long walks across timeless bays,
The distant thunder of the sea
As it hurls itself against the treacherous rocks.
Mountains and mists,
Fine rain like fairy fingers touching your face,
Sing softly, the sunsets are glorious,
The evening star seems to twinkle
With happiness,
As eveningly shyly draws her veils
Across the sky.
Come to Wales
For solace, a deep happiness
And laughter
Come home.

Gwyneth Williams

THANK YOU GOD

Thank you God for a nice warm bed,
Thank you God that I am fed,
Thank you God for the roof above,
Thank you God for I have love
Given to me and that I give,
Thank you God that I live.

K M Dick

TO THE BRIDE AND GROOM

Throughout the coming years
I hope much happiness they hold
Free from those untold fears
Your love together will enfold.

That any trouble you may meet
Be banished and soon solved
You two each dawn may greet
Fresh joys which are untold.

As the years may come and go
Your love may become deeper
Freedom from want, good fortune to flow
And age be the final reaper.

J Wright

COMFORT

Floating in the warm wet
a subdued sense of completeness.
Floating at peace.
The world unaware of the vastness of one
gathered in the only thing you've ever known,
unaware of light, or beware,
in your endless ocean.
Lonely but content.
Secure in the thought of a dark eternity,

But harsh reality comes all too quickly.
Through a tunnel then, light

Naomi Westerman (12)

FRIENDS

Here comes my friend,
My friend?
My friend?
Someone who likes computers,
Someone who lends,
Like tapes and things,
That he will bring,
On a cold Monday morning.

Today my friend and I are going into town,
We'd want to look around,
So if you can see,
My friend and me, we
Are going into town.

He must like,
Reading books,
Playing crooks,
Having looks,
In shops,
But most of all you see
He must be like me.

Royston Elmer (9)

THE SILENT CRY

The moon so bright,
lights up this cold murderous night.
The mournful song sweeps across the ever changing seas.
She calls for her young calf,
and soon he joins her afraid of what might be.

The day had broken,
the wet gleaming off of her skin like coat.
As she surfaced and exhaled the water to breath in once more,
she sensed they were not alone as before.
Fear struck her, she felt her calf by her side,
he seemed to know what she was thinking and sighed.

Seagulls hovered not far away,
suddenly darting into the water as though to say
danger not far from you,
but I'm afraid there's not much we can do.
A sudden cry from the ship came cutting through the air,
there she blows over there.

The story is nearly over I'll let you guess the rest,
for I will always, always love the whales the best.
The cries still go on and on . . . and on . . .
Lets hope the killings soon will have gone.
So now this story is finished and I hope you will all agree,
lets leave them alone in their glorious deep blue sea.

Tracey Lyn Blaker

ON THE DAY I WAS BORN

On the day I was born
The sea was roaring
A child laughed at play
In the city chimney's belched out smoke
An old woman sat in front of the fire
Rivers froze over
Planets blew out flames
A bird fed its babies
An army fought in a battle
My mother cried with happiness.

Laura Stoney (9)

ROCK THE DREAM BOAT

I am the captain of this ship:
I can do anything

I fight the angry waves
& whip the hurricanes
& insult the storm

I plough uneven fields of blueness
& reap their forbidden fruits

I enslave winged creatures
among the mist of my mind
mercilessly.

I am in charge:
in dream-tinted sleep
may I not be
touched.

Gaetana Trippetti

HOWARD THE COWARD

There was a ghost called Howard,
Who believe it or not was
A bit of a coward!

He lived in an old house
Which he shared with
Henry, a little grey mouse.

Henry lived under the floor,
And life for him was
Just never a bore.

At night when the house was quiet,
Henry would explore every room
Looking for cheese, his favourite diet.

But poor old Howard took fright,
When his reflection he saw
In the hall mirror one night!

Now he shakes with fear
Every time that nightfall
Starts to draw near.

Brian Walker

HANDS

Such tiny hands
The baby lying there
Just three days old
Yet clutching and gripping.
Speaking, walking
These two must be delayed
But nature gives to hands
An early strength.

And so confirms
Early both the need
For strength and use of hands.

The musician
Gifted with many skills
The sportsman too
Excelling in his sport.
And every man
May also have beauty
With strength, nature
Cares not from whence or where.

And then too soon
Now three score years and ten
Those hands once strong
With beauty intertwined
Have changed with age.
Disfigured with disease
And painful too.
Just memories remain.

Collin West

LET THERE BE PEACE FOR ALL

Let not their valour crumble
Their strength and courage fade,
Voice once again your praise for peace -
With Christian accolade.

Remember those who gave their life -
So we could walk in peace,
Voice now you gratitude in prayer -
Give thanks for our release.

Malcolm Wilson Bucknall

OUR SAVIOUR

Oh God! Oh God! You had such mercy and love,
And sent your only son from the great above,
He was born to receive terrible hostility and scorn,
And to bear our sins as painful as that ring of thorn.

Ah death! Ah death! Once my dreaded foe,
My friend and saviour Jesus has helped me to know,
That mortality and suffering are not here to stay,
And come the day - that loving hand will lead me away.

Hurrah! Hurrah! It is again Christmas day,
And I now know there is no leading astray.
For Christ's spirit is here for ever and ever
Because I will not leave Christ now for ever!

Amen.

Jonathan Brewer

CHRISTIAN VALUES

What direction do I take?
Which decision should I make?
Who will guide me through the years?
Why must faith mean blood and tears?

Shall religion equal wars?
Guns and bombs promote the cause
Shall the meek inherit earth?
Pain and profit replace mirth.

Join together, form a line
Solidarity of mind
Light a candle, say a prayer
Show mankind that we all care.

Light the hope in children's eyes
Wipe the war planes from the skies
Christians we dare not cease
In our efforts for world peace.

C Robinson

SUMMER

Summer is a time when the birds come out to sing
with the tweeting of their tune
when the spoon of ice-cream goes in.
When the summer leaves are green
when the flower buds are open
when lovely grass is green
when winter time is over.

Summer is a time when summer clothes are out
when the beach is always full
when the pools are nice and cool
when the sun shines so bright.
And the night is always light
when everyone is happy again
because winter time has gone.

Aisha Asamany (8)

CHEWING GUM

I was coughing, I was choking,
My chum said I should give up smoking.
How could my addiction be overcome?
By chewing gum said my chum.
More to please than with belief
I sought chewing gum relief.
Chewing by day - chewing by night
First on the left side - then on the right.
In bus queues standing there and waiting
I resembled a cow ruminating!
Chewing gum from early morning -
Until I got that fatal warning.
About to dispose of some worn-out gum
I did perchance to see
A portion of amalgam
Glaring up at me.
Grasping a mirror I looked to see
Where there might be a cavity;
In actual fact, there were three!
'Oh dear' said my chum,
'That is very rum,
But I've heard of it before,
The same thing happened to my mum
And to the man next door.'
So now I sit in the dentist's chair
Wishing to be anywhere but there
Wishing I had a fag to steady my nerves
Wishing my chum gets what she deserves!

Eileen Greene

ETERNITY

Today I saw eternity
It lit the sky with golden brown
And over sparkled green,
Its light shone a gentle power
And let out heat as if the sun
Into the darkest night.

I knew I'd seen eternity
Because I'd seen the burning light
That reached the tallest sky.
I hadn't known the shape of it
It looked a thousand times the sun
And yet was like the moon.

From now I'll know eternity
And yet I'll see it not again
But keep it always here
For it's my friend, eternity,
And though it reached the tallest sky
It will bend down to me.

R Sumner (13)

WHO CARES?

Can God really be out there?
In a world that's full of despair
The poverty, cruelty and hatred
Why? Surely no-one can care.

The violence we see on the street
The elderly frightened to meet
Pain, hurt and suffering
Does God stand back in defeat?

The bad things in life are man made
In many a way we're afraid
to seek out a God who is there
Who gave his life, our debts paid.

So yes, God really is out there
With his strength and love so rare
Just take the time to find him
You'll then know God truly does care.

Amanda Keefe

TWENTY FIVE YEARS ON

Together we've loved together we've laughed,
And walked the length of love's sweet path,
Now turning a corner of twenty five years,
The future holds no doubts or fears,

Year one we began to sow the seeds,
That brought about these fruitful years,
We cultivated our love and urged it on,
Like flowers and the soil our love became one.

Now as tall as a tree we watch it grow,
Summer, winter, spring and fall,
It's true when they say love conquers all.

Barbara Thomas

CELEBRATION

Powdery sunlight seeps, warms,
Distils pollen,
Magicks stems,
Bursts sticky buds
           to vibrant, twitching stipple-green!

Springy snowdrops jab their heads up,
Puncture iron hard ground,
Gleam like tiny, incandescent torches,
Glitter the valleys, parks and gardens!

Horse Chestnut swaggers, swells;
brandishes its lofty candelabras.
In silent, hanging morning,
rustles a symphony of leaves!

As high above
in glint-blue jigsaw sky,
a solitary blackbird whistles -
celebrating birth, rebirth,
the glorious return of spring!

Jan Porter

A VERY RIDICULOUS POEM ABOUT CHEWING GUM

When I am chewing gum
If I put my hand in my mouth
It gets stuck on my thumb.
And then it causes me grief,
Because it gets stuck on my false teeth
When I was small my Mummy said
Don't swallow gum or else you will be dead.
But now I am older
I've got a lot bolder
I can please myself what I do
As round and round my teeth I chew
Ready to pop in another bit that's new.
And when my teeth go in the cup at night
The gum stays with them out of sight
Ready to start another day.
If the Steradent hasn't dissolved it
Somewhere along the way.

J Potter

CHEWING GUM

Chewing gum, grey and thin,
Peel the wrapper, pop it in,
I asked my Dad, can I have that?
But he said no, turned me down flat,
But why, I said, I want to know,
He said the words that meant no go,
No chewing gum, grey and thin,
No peel the wrapper, pop it in,
He said, in your mouth no such thing,
Because it's made of elephant's skin!

Madge Parker

A PRAYER FROM PRUE

Naughty Prue is saying her pray'rs.
Please God push my dad down the stairs.
He has sent me to bed
Without any tea,
And all because I said
You silly old b - - -

Please give grandad a horrible fright
And set his bushy old whiskers alight,
'Cause he is no fun at all;
But I did blame the cat
When it was me in the hall
That wee-ed in his hat.

Please make mummy baldheaded and plain
To teach her never to slap me again
When all I did was to spit . . .
Oh, mummy's brought me a cake
And my dressing up kit.
Sorry God - it's all a mistake!

Bernard Shough

THE ALL DAY BREAKFAST

O magnificent euphemism!
O tingling sense of guilt!
O surreptitious thrill!

There's nothing, ever, tastes like that;
There's nothing, nowhere, smells like that.
The golden crunch of that f'ed slice;
Hot, sumptuous fat in back of throat;
Rich crackling bacon 'tween the teeth;
The huge, bright yellow eggs; and beans,
With mushrooms, grilled tomatoes,
Sausages and black pudding -
O my joy!

No other satisfaction equal has;
Such calorific glow can nowhere else be found.
The *heart attack* of breakfast is consumed
And, O, I feel so good.

The day might now be all aglow
If my convictions had their courage shown.

Thank you, Miss, no. Just one black coffee
And a low fat yoghurt, please.
Aaah, me!

John Pottinger

CORRIDOR

Waiting to be called when it is my turn
being patient not restless one day must learn
people do not stop as they seem to hurry by
unknown to them as all they are to I
and will I yet be one of them too
accepted into their company with my own job to do
why is it taking so long behind that closed door?
If only the interview was over, I would give anything for
actually the worst of it is being stuck out here
stifled by the smell of polish and vermeer
distracted, to think of others like me who waited for their call
to sign on the dotted line before being sent out to fall
did they wait while wanting nothing else to do?
Or did they wait while knowing that survivors were few?
The pay's not that good and the hours are long
the people here look so miserable, I think I was wrong
let's check out that vacancy in this morning's bulletin
time to go before being asked to come in.

Kevin Corley

THE CONTENTS OF HIS LOCKER

There were a conker the size of a pea
And a white plastic spoon for if he had tea.
A girlie photo showing her bum
And a library book stuck up with gum
There were a bus ticket that cost two quid
He were going to go
But he never did.
And a bitty jumper he swiped
From their kid.
A dog earned timetable for lessons
He hates
And a grubby birthday card for
One of his mates
He is a lazy lad with a future
Not bright
He should shut the door and keep
It all out of sight.

M Ward

THE LAST TIME

The last time I went to the barbers,
I waited on hard upright chairs.
On my turn, the hair was cut
As lots had been that day, that year.
Money paid; event over.
And yet I did not know it was the last time.

The last time I went to the library,
I waited by the black counter.
On my turn, the books were stamped
As part of the hundreds that day, that year.
Books checked; event over.
And yet I did not know it was the last time.

And this is now, and I am here,
In this customary place;
And this time could be the last.

JS

TIME

The hands turn,
The day goes.
What do we do?
Where does it go?

The hands turn,
Life continues.
The world swallows
Time like water.

The hands turn,
The seconds tick,
Slowly, surely
Life slips
by.

The hands turn,
Never waiting,
Unsympathetic.
Time goes on.

The hands turn,
They don't care.
'Life's too short,'
The ticks say,
'Fight it back,
Win time over,
Use your life -
And take a
Chance!'

Julia Gillick

HOUSTON CANAL WITHOUT THE LETTER E FOR ENEMY

Mosquitoes usurp stagnant air and suck my blood.
I cannot disarm this backdoor tyrant,
Nor baulk such sly atrocity.
My skin, poison sown, blooms quickly to furious rash.
I fall to itching, scratching, cursing,
And buy potions which do no good at all.
Like that canal, I am host
To hordes of hungry hoodlums.

Henry Hansen

THE PIRATE

This afternoon
I saw this huge fierce looking man,
Black-bearded, tousle-haired,
Six foot five;
Trousers thick-belted,
Impressively paunched.

He could have come swinging
From the rigging
Of a death-locked enemy ship
Through battle smoke
On to a blood soaked deck,
Demonically yelling,
Knife in his teeth,
Death in his eye.

But actually he was walking
On a sunlit breezy afternoon
Through North Walsham
Carrying lettuce and tomatoes
In little plastic bags.

Cliff Godbold

WALES' BID FOR USA 94

The Welsh soccer team,
let's look on,
Skilful players,
Rush, Giggs, Hughes and Saunders are number one.

Superplayers,
A team is born,
Good Captaincy
from Barry Horn.

Good crowds,
And wonder, if we'll be in the news,
That's a hopeful factor,
With players like Hughes.

The last game at home
and what a din!
We didn't qualify
Don't criticise poor Bodin.

Missed a penalty,
Didn't qualify neither,
But it's not that bad,
England didn't either!

Rowan Belojica

UNTITLED

If we stayed in a place called fear
It would grow into a jungle
Leaving us bewildered
And only creating more of the same
With strange creatures and noises
Hemmed in by the trees.

You could hack out a path
Knowing soon to be free
Fearing each footstep
That brings you nearer to me
On the plains I have waited
I couldn't follow you in . . .

Bewilder my mind or my senses,
But my heart will not sin.

J Whitworth

RIGHT TO LIVE

I heard the scratching and the clawing
Down the embankment, but nothing to see.
My dog busily nosing, what could it be?
I heard it again and searched through the grasses.
And then it was there, a wee baby mole;
Quite the tiniest one I ever had seen.
His night was to live, but oh, in such danger.

Traffic on the road was heavy and quick,
Concrete was under the soil he was clawing.
To live was his right, and he let me uplift him
And take him down to the small copse below.
Off he scuttled away, and how I did hope for him.

Next night I walked by, he was there again.
So this time I carried him further afield
To where moles abounded, and hoped they would find him.
Next night no sign of him, not a sight anywhere.
I searched the road, no view of a victim.
So here, little wild thing, here's to your life.

N Williams

THE FORD
(At Rotten End Wethersfield)
For Lottie Lipton

I stand above you on the bridge,
Where your waters meet the lane
And form a cross;
And in your ageless face see
Roman soldiers at your side.
In your round smooth pebbles
I see David fell Goliath.
Mirrored in your cool clear waters
Lie the countless memories of
Those who, unknowingly, have
Touched the hand of God.

John Wiltshire

GREEN FINGERS

My plants are dancing on the bed.
Making noises like trains and birds.
Their leaves are turning into gold.
So, I'll be rich tomorrow.
No more work for me.
I'll be flying to Spain, and sitting on a donkey.
My plants and I, will be friends forever.
They don't moan, and groan, about the news and weather.

Kenneth Mood

I BELIEVE

I looked on the face of my Grandson today
He is no longer here, he has gone away
Away, where there is no strife
Away to another better life
He knows more than me, although I'm old
Somewhere lovely, we are always told
No trouble at all, was that dear boy
He gave us all a lot of joy
Where's the boy? I would often say
I'm here Gran-ma, so quiet he would play
He was lent to us for twenty years
Will someone wipe away our tears
He will always be young, when we remember him
His eyes will never, ever go dim
And when it is my turn to go, he will say
I'm here Gran-ma, come and play.

Marjorie Davies

MY SPECIAL PRAYER

Help me to be good Lord.
Help me find the way.

Help me to be thoughtful,
As I live from day to day.

Show me what to do Lord.
Show me how to pray.
Show me how to thank you.
Each and every day.

Don't let me speak unkind Lord.
And make somebody cry.

Don't let me pass the other side,

When poverty, I spy.
Let me follow you Lord
And do all you ask,
And Lord, if you will help me,
I can complete my task.

Jacqueline Claire Davies

PERFECTION

I wanted perfection to offer to God.
I strove to advance in His way.
I tried to live up to the ideals I had.
To follow my Lord every day.

I tried hard to earn the salvation I craved.
It was difficult; often I erred.
And I then had a need to begin once again
And try harder to obey his word.

But I found that the time passed; still harder I tried.
I could not be free of my sin.
Then I looked at My Lord on the cross and I knew
That He died, my salvation to win.

I now had perfection to offer to God.
Not earned by my efforts so small.
My faith in the sacrifice Jesus had made
Was accepted, sufficient for all.

Joyce M Turner

A ROSE

The sweetest flower that blows,
I give to you as we part.
For you it's a rose,
For me it's my heart.

It grows in the hearts,
Of those who love.
It's different from all others,
It stands up above.

Its perfume fills the air,
Its fragrance makes you think.
Its petals have a drowsiness;
Which make you smile, love and wink.

Its smell is forever,
Its colour will never fade.
It'll help him remember
The promises he made!

Eram Latif (15)

137

THE BARREN WINTER

It was once life within me,
Like a flower that never blossomed,
Touched by winter's cold hands,
Never to see this world of ours.

The tall city buildings over shadow me,
As if bent over looking down at me,
Once again I am departing, something, a
Part of me, this time it is the city.

Through the steamed train windows
I see vivid images of what I have left
Behind. I am left with memories like
Broken glass, shattered desires.

It is another bitter winter,
The ground is smothered in snow.
Stray rooks line the treetops,
Suffering and starving.

We withdraw from a foggy wood,
Whose trees gave no shelter for my
Guilt. Thought torments my living.
Your future was just a thought.

Habib Naqvi

THE RACE

Stretching muscles
Jogging on the spot
Adrenaline pumping
Walking over to the start
Making sure your foot's behind the line
Bend low
Block out sound
Aim towards the end
Final adrenalin rush
Someone shouts 'Go!'
Running down the track
Arms flapping at your sides
Have a little peep behind
Legs thudding on the ground
The *finish* is closer, and closer
People shouting 'Come on! Come on!'
Then with a final giant step
The line disappears behind you.

Jenna Brown (14)

THE PHONE

Ring. . . Ring. . . ting. . . ting . . . Reach for the phone
Who can it be? Why Mr Bone from across the way,
'Oh hello and a very good day
       What was that! What did you say!
Mrs Fry has gone away . . .
Left her children for a new man
Tell me more if you can . . .
No!. . . Why . . . Oh deary me
Shocking news, how can this be,'
Whatever next I hear him sigh . . .
'Goodness knows' is my reply.
Time to go dear Mr Bone
Thinks I, as I wonder who next to phone . . .
I put down the phone, then pick it up quick
and dial the number of Mrs Flick,
Phone's engaged, who can it be?
I guess it's Mr Bone, who has phoned before me!

T A Reynard

TELEPHONE BELLE

It's quiet on this shelf as I sit by myself,
Waiting for something to happen;
I'm incredibly bored 'til a call from Aunt Maud
Sends a plea for more help down at Clapham.
It's her teeth or her gout or her hair falling out,
But never the call that I long for;
Though plastic and flat, I'm as live as a cat
And dream of the past with nostalgia.
I've loved 'til it hurts the man at the works,
I think that his name was Elvirez,
And I've tried everything to give him a ring,
But can't get through to Enquiries.

Christine Camero

TREVOR'S SONG (HE'S A GOOD ONE)

I have a friend, he isn't real
But I'd like to think so
He's a good one, he's a good one I say.

He lives in peace, he doesn't steal
He keeps away from bad things
He's a good one, he's a good one I say.

Life is short, but still we make it bad
When we take each day, then we make each week,
Like one never had.

If he could speak, what would he feel
About the way we're living?
He's a good one, he's a good one I say,
And he'd say I'm a good one, I'm a good one he'd say.

Life is short, but still we make it bad
When we take each month, then we make each year
Like one never had.

Be like my friend, let's make him real
Oh, let's try to be so
Be a good one, be a good one I say,
Then you'd say, I'm a good one, I'm a good one you'd say!
Be a good one, be a good one today.

Graham Mitchell

WHISPERS . . .

Loch Ness,
Loch Ness,
How you hide the depth,
Deep down inside your mass,
Hiding a secret from your past,
Never knowing, will it be your last,

Where do you hide,
Where can you be,
One day will you be free,
From the cameras and whispering trees,

Where do you go,
What do you seek, As you travel
in your peace,
Will it end if you are found,
No more secrets laying around,

At the hand of man, Will they
grab and take all that they can,
Destroy the magic, hope or myth,
Ruin a dream of peace and calm,
After all you did no harm.

Edwina Gargan Winrow

LET'S GET BACK TO BASICS

Let's get back to basics for all of human kind
Let's get back to basics with common-sense in mind
Let's get back to basics *humanity* the key
Let's get back to basics let's seek *humanity*

Let's get back to basics let's go back to the start
Let's get back to basics put horse before the cart
Let's get back to basics and use our common sense
Let's get back to basics with our intelligence

Let's get back to basics to when our world began
Let's get back to basics to start of species man
Let's get back to basics and try to see some light
Let's get back to basics and try to do it right

Let's get back to basics with *humanity* inside
Let's get back to basics *humanity* our guide
Let's get back to basics for little you and me
Let's get back to basics for all *humanity.*

R Grant

PUR-RING

Pick me up gently
Cradle me in your hands
Touch my parts with care
Hold me near to you
Put your mouth close to mine
Speak gently to me
I like a real smooth operator
Listen to my purring
Try not to get our wires crossed
Don't be angry if you sleep and I wake you
Or if I sometimes make the wrong noises
Be patient if I make you wait
If possible take me with you sometimes
I have a thing about being mobile
If we don't always connect be understanding
You know you can call on me in an emergency
I suppose we could even get engaged
For my dream is to have your ring
You surely have my number.

For I am your telephone.

Purr Purr
purr purr.

Hazel Smith

145

I REMEMBER, I REMEMBER

I remember, I remember,
The little dreamy school,
I always loved to see my friends
The summer dresses cool,
We played outside and had such fun
Under the cherry tree
We always liked our art and craft
My friend Vicky and me.

I remember, I remember,
I never had a care
The life I led was fun for me
But now joy is more rare,
I have to work both day and night
Sometimes I wonder why,
I never seem to get a break
It makes me want to cry.

Lydia Hardcastle

THE KITTEN

Once there was a kitten so good to see,
Play to her was a treat,
She turned and twisted around the floor,
Layed down and went to sleep,
When she woke she was in someone's arms,
It was her owner,
She twitched her nose and went to sleep again,
Purring louder.

Master Aaron J Lumb